SEEKING
SHALOM

PARTICIPANT'S GUIDE

HOW REIMAGINING OUR RESPONSE TO POVERTY CAN
TRANSFORM LIVES AND RESTORE COMMUNITIES

BY SHAWN DUNCAN

DIRECTOR, THE LUPTON CENTER

THANK YOU.

Thank you to the brilliant people who gave of their time and expertise to be interviewed for this project, to the talented folks at SeMA Films and Evangela Creative, to the gifted and generous members of The Lupton Center Task Force who gave life and shape to Seeking Shalom, and to the staff and leadership at FCS | Focused Community Strategies for their innovative and winsome commitment to seeking the Shalom of the city to which God has called them.

"THE OPPOSITE OF POVERTY IS NOT WEALTH, IT IS SHALOM."

STEVE CORBETT, Author, *When Helping Hurts*

TABLE OF CONTENTS

FOREWORD

THE POVERTY NEEDLE IS STUCK. For all of the food we distribute, clothes we give out, and hours and dollars we invest in service projects and mission trips, one would expect that the materially poor would be emerging from poverty. Why is there so little measurable change?

The good news is that a movement is stirring that is raising that very question! Seasoned practitioners are searching for more effective approaches to alleviate poverty, signaling a new day of accountability for service providers. The challenge laying before us is how to change widely accepted practices that deplete dignity to effective paradigms that partner with the materially poor for long-term solutions.

This is the challenge that *Seeking Shalom* addresses.

Through frank, sometimes unsettling personal interviews with people whose knowledge of poverty ranges from homeless shelters to Biblical scholarship, this series confronts common presuppositions that have misguided our work for millennia. Such candid behind-the-scenes glimpses portray a reality seldom heard by compassionate volunteers. This dynamic series advances core principles that, if applied, will dramatically alter our traditional paradigms, leading to the kind of impact we've been eager to see!

Seeking Shalom explores why the poverty needle has been stuck and what it will take to get it moving in a positive direction. If you are willing to apply what this series offers, Shalom — God's peace, prosperity, and well-being — will be extended in generous portion to the marginalized of our world, to the end that all of the human family might flourish and prosper.

BOB LUPTON

Author, Toxic Charity
Founder, FCS | Focused Community Strategies

NOTE TO THE PARTICIPANT

FIRST, LET ME SAY THANK YOU.

You have responded to an invitation to join others in wrestling with what it means to respond to God's call to care for those experiencing poverty. Thank you! You and your small group or class have the opportunity to work together to change the way your community responds to material poverty.

Second, I want you to know who is behind *Seeking Shalom*. This series was created by The Lupton Center, a training and consulting organization working with groups all over the country who, like you, are actively seeking ways to change the paradigm for charity. We are not a publishing business; we are a practitioner's organization. Our day-to-day work is focused on what is happening in the neighborhoods and cities around the US and world where material poverty is present. We would love to connect with you through our website, social media, or in person at a training event!

Finally, take full advantage of this Participant's Guide. There are pages to help you participate fully in the weekly class sessions, and there are additional reflection and application exercises you can do throughout the week. *Seeking Shalom* is about much more than videos for discussion; this series can transform the way your community understands and responds to material poverty.

I look forward to hearing from you soon!

Many Blessings,

SHAWN DUNCAN
Director, The Lupton Center
www.LuptonCenter.org

WHAT WENT WRONG WITH DOING GOOD?

KEY IDEA

The church has been faithful to the biblical mandate to love those experiencing poverty, but our methods have not been effective. The traditional paradigm is expressed in models that are often not based in relationship and have not distinguished between crisis and chronic poverty. When the problems are not accurately understood, it leads to ineffective and, at times, harmful actions.

LEARNING OBJECTIVES:

- To understand that the traditional paradigm for addressing material poverty is not working
- To understand the importance of proximity
- To understand the need to distinguish between crisis and chronic poverty

"So many of our traditional charity models provide a lot of activities and services...people have fuller bellies and a warm place to sleep at night, which are really good, but that does not change the trajectory of anyone's life. Our common charity models have provided comfort to poverty but have not come any closer to ending poverty."

Katie Delp, *Executive Director, FCS | Focused Community Strategies*

Jesus went to Nazareth, where he had been brought up, and on the Sabbath day he went into the synagogue, as was his custom. He stood up to read, and the scroll of the prophet Isaiah was handed to him. Unrolling it, he found the place where it is written:

"The Spirit of the Lord is on me,
  because he has anointed me
  to proclaim good news to the poor.
He has sent me to proclaim freedom for the prisoners
  and recovery of sight for the blind,
to set the oppressed free,
  to proclaim the year of the Lord's favor."

Then he rolled up the scroll, gave it back to the attendant and sat down. The eyes of everyone in the synagogue were fastened on him. He began by saying to them, "Today this scripture is fulfilled in your hearing." -Luke 4:18-20 (NIV)

KEY IDEA

SEEKING SHALOM WILL show how that the traditional _____ for addressing material poverty is not leading to the _____ that we would like to see. Seeking Shalom will celebrate our compassion and generosity but question the paradigm by which we often express them.

SEEKING SHALOM WILL build a robust _____ framework for understanding poverty. Seeking Shalom will help us to understand what the Bible means by poverty and point us toward more impactful _____ of engagement.

SEEKING SHALOM WILL share _____ core principles for shaping healthy ways of engaging material poverty. Seeking Shalom is interested in seeing lives transformed and communities restored. It will not offer blueprint for a program to replicate, but it will show you these core principles are essential for addressing whatever issues your community is facing.

VIDEO

As you view this week's first video, *"Is Charity Working?"*, write down any quotes, terms, or ideas that you find meaningful. Record any thing you learn about why some methods for addressing material poverty are ineffective or harmful.

Thinking about the church that first introduced you to the Christian faith, which of the following options best reflects your experience.

An active participation in the lives of those experiencing poverty was:

<table>
<tr>
<td>

Rarely talked about or practiced. There seemed to be little connection between this and Christian orthodoxy or identity.

</td>
<td>

Occasionally practiced and talked about. It was honored as a good thing for Christians to do, but was not treated as an expectation for authentic faith.

</td>
</tr>
<tr>
<td>

Often talked about and practiced. Though it was emphasized, it was treated more like an addition to Christian faith but not central to following Jesus.

</td>
<td>

Almost always talked about and practiced. An active participation in the lives of those experiencing poverty was treated as an inseparable part of Christian identity.

</td>
</tr>
</table>

DISCUSSION QUESTIONS

- Do you feel like this portrayal accurately reflects the biblical testimony?

- Have volunteers read James 1:27 and Matthew 25:34-40.

- Do you feel these passages are evidence that being a Christian by definition means actively caring for those experiencing poverty?

- Do you think we tend see poverty as a cause that certain people feel called to rather than something the whole church should care about? If so, why do you think we do that?

THE BIBLE not only has a clear

_____ for alleviating

material poverty; it is also concerned that

our _____ are both healthy

and effective.

We often talk about the importance of the motives behind our actions. We know that the Bible is concerned with our hearts being in the right place when we serve, give, or express care for another person. We also know that the Bible clearly mandates that followers of Jesus, like Jesus Himself, are to actively serve those experiencing poverty. From cover to cover the Bible shows that God and God's people are concerned about mercy, compassion, and justice for those experiencing poverty. We cannot miss, though, that God's Word is also clearly concerned with the ways in which we obey this mandate. Just as we are concerned with obedience and right motives, we also have to be concerned that our methods lead to the results that God's desires.

EXERCISE

1. Read and follow the instructions in the left column on the following page.

2. After you have read the passage, share a summary and your reflections with the group.

3. Once you have finished, proceed to the right column.

BIBLICAL TEXTS

Have each person choose one of the passages listed below. Each passage expresses God's mandate for God's people to care about those experiencing poverty. As you read the passage, look for indications of concern about *the way* poverty is addressed.

Gleaning Laws - Lev 19:10;
Hiring Practices - Duet 24:14;
Protection of Rights - Psalm 82:3-4;
Call to Freedom - Isaiah 58:6-7

BIBLICAL PRINCIPLES

On this side of the page, list any biblical principles that may not directly address poverty but offer evidence that our methods for engaging poverty matter to God.

For example, if we know the Bible calls us to "love our neighbor as ourselves," then we could argue that the Bible commands us to treat the materially poor as equals and with dignity. Write your own ideas and share with your Circle.

VIDEO

As you view *"Why Isn't Charity Working?"* write down any quotes, terms, or ideas that you find meaningful. Record anything you learn about why some methods for addressing material poverty are ineffective or harmful.

KEY IDEA

- The first major issue with traditional charity models is that they suffer from a _____ _____ . This is the geographic and relational distance between those giving and those receiving. This distance does not allow us to understand the problems accurately and design effective solutions.

> "This idea of having a more relational, rather than transactional, encounter isn't new, however. When we pay close attention to the biblical texts that call us to generosity and compassion, they assume there is a personal connection. They assume that the people are living in community with one another. The context of biblical generosity is often hospitality, not service providing."
>
> *From Seeking Shalom: Leader's Guide*

- The second major issue with traditional charity models is that they suffer from a _____ _____ . A failure to distinguish between crisis and chronic poverty will cause us to misapply our compassion, leading to ineffective or harmful solutions. A crisis demands emergency relief. Chronic poverty requires development.

VIDEO

As you view the animated parable *"The Cold Water Collective"* write down any key ideas or thoughts you have.

PRAYER JOURNAL

Write out your prayer for addressing the proximity disorder in your life and within any ministries in which you participate.

Write out your prayer for addressing the diagnostic error that may be affecting ministries in which you are involved.

REFLECTION QUESTIONS

1. Take a moment to look back over your notes from Day One: Class Day. What do you think are your most important takeaways from the first session?

_____

_____

_____

_____

2. In your own words, finish this statement: Charity is ineffective or harmful when...

_____

_____

_____

_____

3. The first session talked about the need to distinguish between crisis and chronic poverty. List a few examples of each.

_____

_____

_____

_____

SCRIPTURE MEDITATIONS

The passage for study and meditation today is Luke 4:14-21. Luke chose this moment in a synagogue in Nazareth to be the first time we would hear Jesus speak publicly. What is interesting is that, if you were to construct a timeline of Jesus' life, this moment would not be found anywhere near the starting point. This means that Luke did not place this text at the beginning his Gospel for chronological purposes. Luke put this passage first for theological reasons.

1. Carefully read Luke 4:14-21. Why do you think Luke chose this as the moment to inaugurate the public ministry of Jesus in his Gospel?

2. This passage is Jesus's own declaration of why God sent him — like his own personal mission statement. In your own words, what does Jesus say the Spirit has commissioned him to do?

3. Luke makes it clear that engaging oppression, poverty, and suffering are not secondary to the mission of Jesus. And Luke did not write this passage or the rest of his Gospel just for historical purposes. He wasn't just giving us a factual narrative about Jesus. Luke wrote a story with an audience in mind - the Church. Luke wrote to tell us about our own identity. Reread verses 18 & 19 aloud and replace the "me's" in verse 18 with the name of your church.

4. Reread it aloud and replace the "me's" with your own name.

5. Now meditate carefully on verses 18 & 19. Read each individual phrase of these verses with a significant pause between each one. Pray and listen to what God may be saying to you about why the Spirit has placed you where you are.

CASE STUDY

This week's Case Study will be further reflection about *The Cold Water Collective*, the animated parable that you viewed this week during Session One. Read over the script from that parable and answer the questions that follow.

A certain woman felt called by God to serve the poor and the vulnerable. Upon hearing of God's heart for the marginalized, she was moved to compassion knowing that her bucket was full, while many people lived with empty buckets. She could hear Jesus calling her to share generously cups of cold water with the poor. So, one day she decided to go to a place where people lived with empty buckets. She poured from her abundance so they could have full buckets too. This woman was so blessed by making a difference, she decided to keep doing this. And she did. Every week. For years. Eventually, she gathered her friends who also had full buckets, told them about this amazing ministry, and they joined her to form the Cold Water Collective — people who would draw from their own abundance, travel to places of emptiness, and fill the buckets of the least of these. From 10 buckets a week in one neighborhood, to 100 buckets a week in 5 neighborhoods to, by their tenth year, 1,000 buckets a week across 45 locations. The Cold Water Collective was hailed as a success. Until one day, I asked, "Have you ever wondered why, after years of pouring from your buckets into mine, your buckets remain full and mine remains empty?"

1. When you reread this story, what most concerns you about *The Cold Water Collective?*

2. What details about *The Cold Water Collective* stuck out to you that you may not have noticed prior to the videos and conversations from Session One?

_____

_____

_____

_____

_____

3. Knowing what you know now about the the Proximity Disorder, what would you say should have been done differently when the woman in the story became aware of those empty buckets and felt prompted to respond?

_____

_____

_____

_____

_____

4. Knowing what you know now about the the Diagnostic Error, what would you say should have been done differently when the woman in the story became aware of those empty buckets and felt prompted to respond?

_____

_____

_____

_____

_____

5. Take a few minutes and rewrite *The Cold Water Collective's* story the way you think it should have gone.

VIDEO

The Lupton Center has curated additional online video content available exclusively to Seeking Shalom participants. This week you have the privilege of hearing from Julia Dinsmore as she tells the story behind and recites for us her famous poem, "My Name is Not Those People."

To view this video, go to **LuptonCenter.org/SSResources** and use the password: **ShalomSeeker**. Choose the video entitled, *"Session One: My Name."* After watching the video, answer the questions below.

1. What emotions did you experience as you heard Julia's story and listened to her poem?

2. Have you ever had the experience of being "othered" — seen as a category or being depersonalized with a label like "those people?"

3. When have you found yourself "othering" — seeing people as a category or depersonalizing them with labels like "those people?"

_____

_____

_____

_____

_____

_____

4. Often, when we become aware of flaws in the current charity paradigm, we focus on fixing things within the program itself. Julia's poem highlights the part that gets overlooked — the proximity disorder. We have to address the relational distance that causes those who want to serve or help to see the people they want to help as less than the full bearers of God's image that they are. Write out your prayers and your ideas about how to address the relationship gap and any resulting unhealthy perspectives that exist in your life and ministry.

_____

_____

_____

_____

_____

_____

WHAT DOES THE BIBLE SAY ABOUT POVERTY?

KEY IDEA

It is well known that the Bible has a lot to say about poverty and that it reveals God's overwhelming concern for those experiencing it. However, how the Bible defines poverty or frames its causes is not as commonly known. The Bible does not present one single definition or cause, but reveals multiple ways to define poverty and a wide variety of reasons why it might exist. This week, we are invited to take a more holistic view of poverty within a relational framework and to identify its many dimensions.

LEARNING OBJECTIVES:

• Participants will come to understand that poverty is something we all experience. Material poverty is only one aspect of what is understood in the Bible as poverty. All versions of poverty are the result of broken relationships with God, self, others, systems, and/or the created order.

• Participants will come to understand that Scripture reveals that material poverty is the result of many different interrelated factors. A single-cause, single solution approach will never move the poverty needle.

"Poverty is very complicated. It is not the symptom of one thing. It is the manifestation of a lot of different things. So, in eradicating poverty it is not just a straight line; it is a spectrum. To get to eradicating poverty there is not one way."

Sushma Barakoti, *Clarkston Coordinator | StartME Accelerator Program*

KEY TEXT

"For the Lord your God is God of gods and Lord of lords, the great God, mighty and awesome, who shows no partiality and accepts no bribes. He defends the cause of the fatherless and the widow, and loves the immigrant residing among you, giving them food and clothing." - Deuteronomy 10:17-18

EXERCISE

Free-Association Exercise: The class facilitator will give you a word and a time limit. You are to write as much as possible that comes to mind — images, sounds, feelings, people, places, movies, books, etc. — in that time.

DISCUSSION

Gather with your Circle and discuss the following questions about the Free-Association exercise.

1. What were some of the first and most pressing things that came to mind?

_____

_____

_____

2. What came up that surprised you?

_____

_____

_____

3. What did this exercise teach you about your own perspective on poverty?

_____

_____

_____

4. How much do you think the things you thought about in this free-association exercise influence the way you respond to poverty and those experiencing it?

_____

_____

_____

VIDEO

As you view *"The Bible and Poverty, Part One,"* feel free to write down anything that strikes you along the way. You may want to write down things you hear that relate to the different reasons why the Bible says poverty exists.

A 'SYMPTOMS' UNDERSTANDING OF POVERTY

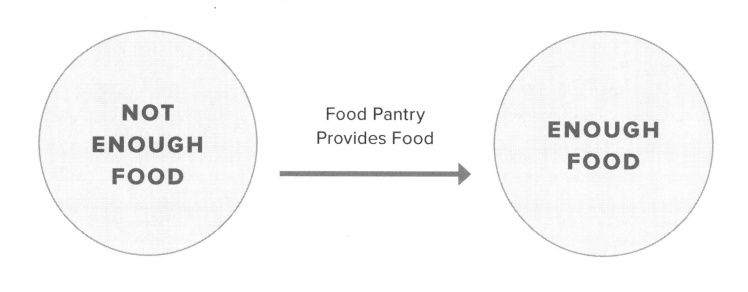

NOT ENOUGH FOOD

Food Pantry Provides Food →

ENOUGH FOOD

A 'SYSTEMS' UNDERSTANDING OF POVERTY

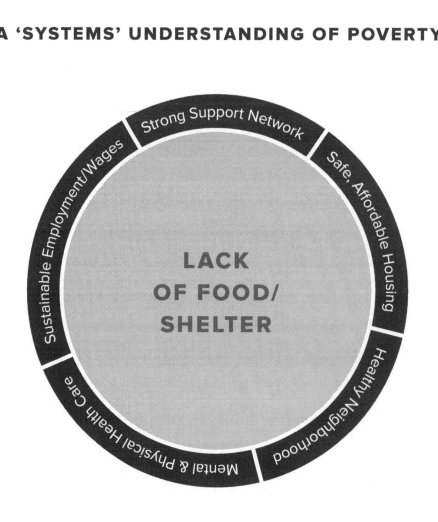

LACK OF FOOD/ SHELTER

Strong Support Network

Safe, Affordable Housing

Healthy Neighborhood

Mental & Physical Health Care

Sustainable Employment/Wages

VIDEO

As you view *"The Bible and Poverty, Part Two"* feel free to write down anything that strikes you along the way. You may want to write down things you hear that relate to the different reasons why the Bible says poverty exists.

"ONE KEY WAY to understand poverty as it is portrayed in the Bible is to pay careful attention to the oft repeated phrase,

' _____ , _____ ,

and _____ .' "

See Deut 16:11, 14; 26:12; Ps 94:6; Jer 22:3; Zech 7:10.

Deuteronomy 10:17-18: [17] For the Lord your God is God of gods and Lord of lords, the great God, mighty and awesome, who shows no partiality and accepts no bribes. [18] He defends the cause of the fatherless and the widow, and loves the foreigner residing among you, giving them food and clothing.

Zechariah 7:8-12: [8] And the word of the Lord came again to Zechariah: [9] "This is what the Lord Almighty said: 'Administer true justice; show mercy and compassion to one another. [10] Do not oppress the widow or the fatherless, the foreigner or the poor. Do not plot evil against each other.' [11] "But they refused to pay attention; stubbornly they turned their backs and covered their ears. [12] They made their hearts as hard as flint and would not listen to the law or to the words that the Lord Almighty had sent by his Spirit through the earlier prophets. So the Lord Almighty was very angry.

"THE WIDOW, orphan, and immigrant lack a _____ in the management of social power." - Walter Brueggemann

REASONS FOUND IN THE BIBLE WHY MATERIAL POVERTY EXISTS

Key Idea: The Bible Does Not Present a Single Cause or Single Solution.

- **Crises:** "In the days when the judges ruled, there was a famine in the land." Ruth 1:1

- **Choices:** "The plans of the diligent lead to profit as surely as haste leads to poverty." Prov 21:5

- **Exploitation:** "The wages you have failed to pay the workers are crying out against you. The cries of the harvesters have reached the ears of the Lord Almighty." James 5:4

- **Injustice:** "Woe to those who make unjust laws...to deprive the poor of their rights." Isa 10:1-2

- **Marginalization:** "Do not oppress the widow or the fatherless, the immigrant or the poor." Zech 7:10

Key Idea: These five do not show up in equal measure or carry equal weight in Scripture. The first two have the fewest references, while the final three occur repeatedly throughout the narrative of Scripture.

KEY IDEA

MATERIAL POVERTY in Scripture has much more to do with _____ than it has to do

with _____. A more accurate representation of material poverty would be to define it as

an experience of being _____ rather than being _____.

VIDEO

As we watch the video *"A Relational Framework for Understanding Poverty,"* write down any thoughts or ideas that you find meaningful.

A RELATIONAL FRAMEWORK
FOR UNDERSTANDING POVERTY

As we are "seeking Shalom," the relational framework for understanding poverty can be symbolized as a peace sign. Poverty is the experience when one or more of the relationships experiences a form of brokenness. This framework is adapted from and based on the work of Bryant Myers in *Walking With The Poor* and Fikkert and Corbett in *When Helping Hurts.*

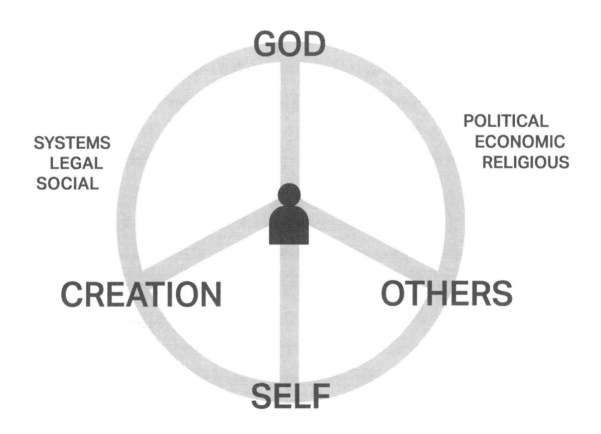

KEY IDEA: If we change our paradigm for understanding poverty from a _____ to a

framework, then we will focus on the practice of _____ rather than the distribution

of _____ . This framework exists because all people have been made in _____ .

PRAYER JOURNAL

Write out your own prayer for practicing the ministry of reconciliation.

Write out your own prayer for seeing and treating all people as bearers of the image of God.

REFLECTION QUESTIONS

1. Take a moment to look back over your notes from Day One: Class Day. What do you think are your most important takeaways from Session Two in Seeking Shalom?

2. Look back at the image on page 40, *"Relational Framework for Understanding Poverty."* Pick a symptom of poverty and then write down three different scenarios that could cause that symptom based on three different relationships symbolized in the graphic.

3. Session Two placed the idea of the image of God front and center in the work to eradicate poverty. If that belief anchored everything we did, what do you think would change?

SCRIPTURE MEDITATION: JAMES

One of the key passages that roots the Christian faith in the practice of loving those experiencing poverty is James 1:27: "Religion that God our Father accepts as pure and faultless is this: to look after orphans and widows in their distress and to keep oneself from being polluted by the world."

James contains two other passages related to material poverty. Some treat these three texts as passages that may be topically related – i.e. dealing with poverty – but not directly correlated. What if we challenged that notion? What if the three texts were meant to be understood together? Read all three passages looking for the collective statement they are making.

- **James 2:1-9**: My brothers and sisters, believers in our glorious Lord Jesus Christ must not show favoritism. [2] Suppose a man comes into your meeting wearing a gold ring and fine clothes, and a poor man in filthy old clothes also comes in. [3] If you show special attention to the man wearing fine clothes and say, "Here's a good seat for you," but say to the poor man, "You stand there" or "Sit on the floor by my feet," [4] have you not discriminated among yourselves and become judges with evil thoughts? [5] Listen, my dear brothers and sisters: Has not God chosen those who are poor in the eyes of the world to be rich in faith and to inherit the kingdom he promised those who love him? [6] But you have dishonored the poor. Is it not the rich who are exploiting you? Are they not the ones who are dragging you into court? 7 Are they not the ones who are blaspheming the noble name of him to whom you belong? [8] If you really keep the royal law found in Scripture, "Love your neighbor as yourself," you are doing right. [9] But if you show favoritism, you sin and are convicted by the law as lawbreakers. to each other.

- **James 5:1-6**: Now listen, you rich people, weep and wail because of the misery that is coming on you. [2] Your wealth has rotted, and moths have eaten your clothes. [3] Your gold and silver are corroded. Their corrosion will testify against you and eat your flesh like fire. You have hoarded wealth in the last days. [4] Look! The wages you failed to pay the workers who mowed your fields are crying out against you. The cries of the harvesters have reached the ears of the Lord Almighty. [5] You have lived on earth in luxury and self-indulgence. You have fattened yourselves in the day of slaughter. [6] You have condemned and murdered the innocent one, who was not opposing you.

1. What connections did you notice when taking these three texts as a whole?

_____

_____

_____

_____

2. How do these passages challenge the paradigm of simply providing material resources to someone experiencing poverty?

_____

_____

_____

_____

_____

3. Carefully read back through all three passages, paying close attention to how the Spirit may be speaking into your own life through these words. Write out your prayer and reflections below.

_____

_____

_____

_____

_____

CASE STUDY

This week's Case Study is a ministry called Abundant Table. Read their story and answer the questions that follow.

Over the last 15 years the churches near a local school noticed significant change in the school's demographics. Intrigued and somewhat delighted by these new languages and faces, they thought hard about how to be good neighbors. Over time, they saw that the online ratings of the school were declining and heard that over 80% of the students received free or reduced lunch. It took a good while for members of these churches to believe that poverty existed nearby. While out for their Saturday bike ride through the neighborhood, three friends, Fernando, Ric, and Marcus, were talking about the school, the changes in the neighborhood, and what their churches should do. Ric wondered aloud, "If kids are on the free lunch program, what do they do during this summer when the school is not there to provide for them?" These men had never thought about that before. They had been blessed to never have to think about that in their own lives. They began to grow impassioned by their shared conviction of God's concern for the poor and for children. They spoke about the visions of God's Kingdom in Scripture of a feast where all freely ate and were filled. By the time the ride was over, they had a plan in mind. They would go to their separate churches and share the vision for Abundant Table — bringing the abundance of the Kingdom feast to one child at a time, one lunch at a time. They would rotate weeks all summer long, making lunches and distributing them from church vans in all the apartment complexes and lower-income neighborhoods around the school. The vision took off in all three churches, and they quickly added two others. Five churches have been working together for the last six years to provide free lunches all summer to the children in the community. Every year the number of kids being served has grown.

1. What concerns about this ministry immediately rose to the surface for you? Circle things that you think are to be celebrated. Underline things that you think are unhealthy.

2. So far in *Seeking Shalom*, we have discussed the following core concepts: Proximity Disorder, Diagnostic Error, Relational Framework for Understanding Poverty, and Image of God. Chose one of these concepts and write down how applying it to Abundant Table would affect the ministry.

_____

_____

_____

_____

3. What are the top 3 things you think they should have done differently from the beginning?

_____

_____

_____

_____

_____

_____

4. Since they can't go back in time and start over, what do you think could be done now to make Abundant Table healthier?

_____

_____

_____

_____

_____

VIDEO

The Lupton Center has curated additional online video content available exclusively to Seeking Shalom participants. This week, you can watch a short animation that revisits the 5 reasons why poverty exists in the Bible.

To view this video, go to **LuptonCenter.org/SSResrouces** and use the password: **ShalomSeeker**. Choose the video entitled, *"Session Two: Five Reasons Animation."* After watching the video, answer the questions below.

1. When you have heard poverty talked about in church, which of these 5 reasons has been either directly or indirectly assumed to be the cause? (Feel free to review by looking at the list on page 37.)

2. Take the idea of food insecurity. Choose three of the 5 reasons as the cause behind the lack of a sustainable, healthy food supply. Write down how each response should be different based on that cause.

3. Considering the fact that the Bible does not offer one cause, definition, or solution to poverty, how should that influence how we respond to a person, family, or community experiencing it?

WHAT IS
THE OPPOSITE
POVERTY?

KEY IDEA

We not only need to consider the causes of a problem, we need to be clear about what we expect the solution to be. The first two sessions encouraged us to consider carefully what factors are causing the observable symptoms of poverty. Discerning the causes, however, is not all that is needed. We need to be clear about our goals. The goals we set will determine the strategies we implement and the things we use to measure success. The Bible invites us to do more than provide a material recourse to alleviate momentary suffering. The Bible invites us to consider that the opposite of poverty is not wealth; it is Shalom. We need to shift from a paradigm concerned with meeting needs to one that is interested in seeking Shalom.

LEARNING OBJECTIVES:

- Participants will discuss and commit to The Oath for Compassionate Helpers as a way of dedicating themselves to healthy standards for serving those experiencing poverty.

- Participants will come to understand that God's vision for humanity is Shalom. Poverty alleviation is not about the provision of material resources where there is lack. It is about ensuring all people have access to sustainable flourishing.

- Participants will come to understand the interrelated factors that the Bible says bring about Shalom.

> "God does not delight in worldly wisdom, power, or money. God delights in neighborly fidelity that is busy constructing the infrastructures of Shalom."
>
> **Walter Brueggemann,** *OT Scholar, Author of* God, Neighbor, Empire

"The thief comes only to steal and kill and destroy; I have come that they may have life, and have it to the full. ~Jesus, John 10:10

THE OATH FOR COMPASSIONATE HELPERS

I will never do for others what they have the capacity to do for themselves.

I will limit one-way giving to crises and seek always to find ways for legitimate exchange.

I will seek ways to empower by hiring, lending, and investing and offer gifts sparingly to celebrate achievements.

I will put the interests of those experiencing poverty above my own (or organizational) self-interest, even when it means setting aside my own agenda.

I will listen carefully, even to what is not being said, knowing that unspoken feelings may contain essential clues to healthy engagement.

Above all, to the best of my ability, I will do no harm.

Gather in your Circle to discuss "The Oath."

1. Reread the text of "The Oath" aloud.

2. Which statement in "The Oath" is most meaningful for you and why?

3. In your opinion, which one of these would be the most difficult to follow? Why?

4. How does "The Oath" connect with the four main concepts we've discussed so far (Proximity Disorder, Diagnostic Error [Crisis vs. Chronic], Relational Framework, and Image of God)?

VIDEO

As you watch the video *"The Opposite of Poverty is not Wealth,"* feel free to take notes and record the things you find meaningful.

DISCUSSION

1. Read the passage the Facilitator assigned to your Circle.

   (a) "The Sheep and Goats" Matt 25:34-36

   (b) "Throwing a Party" Luke 14:12-14

   (c) "The Good Samaritan" Luke 10:25-37

   (d) "Cup of Cold Water" Matthew 10:40-42

2. Do you think your passage justifies the one-way giving paradigm? Or does it model something deeper or more robust?

3. How does this example of meeting the physical need of another person differ from traditional charity models in our day?

2. Thinking again about our four main concepts from Sessions One and Two (Proximity Disorder, Diagnostic Error, Relational Framework, and Image of God), how does your passage relate to what we've learned so far?

RENEWING OUR IMAGINATIONS

CHARITY PARADIGM: The Bible invites us to _____ for others in _____ of need.

SHALOM PARADIGM: The Bible invites us to _____ with God in the renewal of _____.

THE OPPOSITE of poverty is not wealth. It is _____.

What does this mean to you? What biblical passages or images influence how you understand Shalom?

_____

_____

_____

_____

_____

_____

_____

VIDEO

As you watch the video *"The Meaning of Shalom,"* feel free to take notes on things that you find meaningful. Be sure to note anything in the video that helps shape your view of Shalom.

THE INFRASTRUCTURES OF SHALOM

Jeremiah 9:23-24

23 This is what the Lord says:

"Let not the wise boast of their wisdom

or the strong boast of their strength

or the rich boast of their riches,

24 but let the one who boasts boast about this:

that they have the understanding to know me,

that I am the Lord, who exercises kindness,

justice and righteousness on earth,

for in these I delight," declares the Lord.

"God does not _____ in worldly wisdom, power, or money. God delights in _____ fidelity that is busy constructing the _____ of Shalom." -**Walter Brueggemann,** *OT Scholar, Author of* God, Neighbor, Empire

- What does the phrase "infrastructures of Shalom" mean to you?

_____

_____

_____

_____

_____

_____

_____

_____

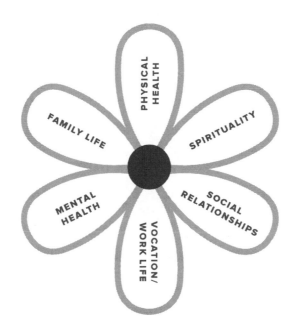

INDIVIDUAL FLOURISHING

Color in each pedal to the degree that you feel you are flourishing in that area.

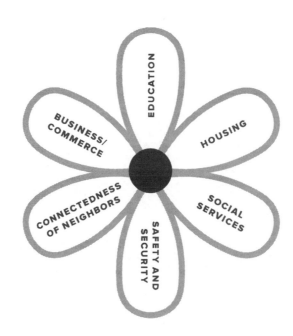

COMMUNITY FLOURISHING

Color in each pedal to the degree that you feel your community is flourishing in that area.

DISCUSSION

1. On the Individual Flourishing image, look at an area where you are not experiencing much flourishing. How would it affect the other 5 areas if that "petal" were to fill up?

2. Similarly, look at an area where you are seeing flourishing. How would it affect the other 5 areas if that "petal" were to empty?

3. On the Community Flourishing image, look at an area where you are seeing flourishing. How would it affect the other 5 areas if that "petal" were to empty?

4. Similarly, look at an area where you are not seeing much flourishing. How would it affect the other 5 areas if that "petal" were to fill up?

5. What is the result of charity efforts that try to address just one area without paying attention to what is happening in others?

6. Similarly, what if we only focus on individuals, even holistically, without thinking about the flourishing of the community as a whole?

SHALOM IS _____.

Therefore, _____

ain't _____ !!

PRAYER JOURNAL

Write out your prayer for God to renew your imagination for seeing God's call for Shalom in Scripture.

Write out your prayers for God to bring about Shalom in the lives of the participants in your class.

Write out your prayer for God to bring about Shalom in the community in which you live.

REFLECTION QUESTIONS

1. Take a moment to look back over your notes from Day One: Class Day. What do you think are your most important takeaways from the third session?

2. In your own words, finish this statement: Shifting paradigms from meeting needs to seeking Shalom means...

3. Where is there a lack of flourishing in your community? How might you or your church participate in seeking Shalom in that area?

4. Where is there a lack of flourishing in your own life? Who has God placed in your life to partner with you in pursuing God's Shalom in that area?

SCRIPTURE MEDITATION

1. Carefully read through Colossians 1:15-20. Reread it aloud with emphasis each time the word **"all"** appears.

2. Why do you think Paul used the word "all" so many times?

3. It is common for Jesus to be seen as the head of religious things — morality, spirituality, church life, etc. It is less common to have this vision of Jesus as the all-encompassing supreme head of all things. Paul shows that Jesus is holding ALL things together, that Jesus is working to reconcile ALL things to God's intended purpose. Why do you think we limit Jesus to caring about religious things?

4. When we do affirm that Jesus cares about physical things, we tend to limit that concern to basic needs like food and shelter. We don't often think that Jesus wants His will to be done in education, health care, housing, legal structure, neighborhood health, etc. Why do you think we limit Jesus's headship to basic necessities?

5. What would it mean if we embraced the call to partner with Jesus as He is working to reconcile ALL things to God?

_____

_____

_____

_____

_____

_____

6. Carefully and prayerfully read Col 1:15-23, opening your heart to awe. Embrace the beauty of the supremacy of Jesus, the work He is doing in you, and the work He is doing in the world.

Write out your response and prayer to Jesus.

_____

_____

_____

_____

_____

_____

CASE STUDY

This week's Case Study will be on a mission effort called *Soul-Full*. Read their story below and answer the questions that follow.

Soul-Full. On the final night of a mission trip to a Central American country, a group of students and adults share what they learned from the trip. One student, Shelby, passionately shared her concern for the number of children she saw running and playing without shoes. She lamented how much she had at home — closets overflowing with clothes and more shoes than she even wears. She was determined to have every kid in that village have a pair of new shoes before school restarted. The adults celebrated her compassion and conviction. Her peers got excited about how this idea could work. Before leaving, they told their host, a farmer who was also the pastor of a small church nearby, what they were going to do. Their hearts were warmed by his generous smile and sincere thank you. Returning home, the group shared their stories, showed pictures, and had Shelby roll out the plan for this new ministry: *Soul-Full* — filling souls with joy by ensuring every child has soles on their feet. When Shelby presented her heartfelt vision, the congregation quickly caught her energy and passion. And the children's shoe donations came pouring in. When they saw the overwhelming response of the church, the leaders of Soul-Full knew that God was blessing this effort. They began to express that they should dream bigger because they served a big God! So for the last five years, *Soul-Full* has been shipping boxes of shoes to pastors of local churches in the villages surrounding the area where they first took that mission trip.

1. Underline key words, phrases, or moments in the story that cause you concern.

2. Choose one or two of them and write out why you are concerned.

_____

_____

_____

_____

3. Is there a central theme or idea that you think defines this particular response to a symptom of poverty?

_____

_____

_____

_____

4. What do you think are the effects of this ministry on the ground in the villages where the donations are sent?

_____

_____

_____

_____

5. Based on what you have learned so far, what could the adults have done differently when Shelby first expressed her concern?

_____

_____

_____

_____

_____

_____

_____

6. How might a paradigm of seeking Shalom respond to this symptom of poverty?

_____

_____

_____

_____

_____

_____

_____

VIDEO

The Lupton Center has curated additional online video content available exclusively to Seeking Shalom participants. This week, you can watch a short animation that revisits the five reasons found in the Bible for the existence of poverty.

To view this video, go to **LuptonCenter.org/SSResrouces** and use the password: **ShalomSeeker**. Choose the video entitled, *"Session Three: Infrastructures of Shalom."*

After watching the video, answer the questions below:

1. Thinking about the 5 things highlighted in the video (Law, Leadership, Generous Solidarity, Image or God, and Radical Hope), which one do you see are being particularity strong in your community?

2. Which one do you feel is lacking? Why?

3. What would you add to that list? If people got busy constructing the infrastructures of Shalom in your community, what else would they need to work on?

4. If you were to work on shaping Shalom in your community, where could you see yourself focusing your energy?

HOW DO WE SEEK SHALOM? PART ONE

KEY IDEA

Shalom is an all-inclusive concept. No part of our lives or this world is exempt from God's vision of bringing about Shalom. This can leave us feeling both inspired and paralyzed. Where do we begin? How do we take practical steps toward something so big? This week we learn that the only context for seeking Shalom is within mutually transformative relationships where all people are welcomed as full participants.

LEARNING OBJECTIVES:

• Participants will come understand that the journey to Shalom begins by entering into mutually transformative relationships. Mutuality is the antidote to the paternalism that often occurs in traditional one-way giving models.

• Participants will come to understand that the journey to Shalom can only be walked when everyone is treated as a full, dignified participant in the process. As long as people are treated as passive recipients defined by their deficiency, Shalom can never be experienced. As bearers of God's image, all people have voices to be heard and gifts to be utilized.

"In development, the community is always the first investor."

Bob Lupton, *Author of* Toxic Charity and Charity Detox

"Now to each one the manifestation of the Spirit is given for the common good."

- 1 Corinthians 12:7

THIS WEEK'S SHALOM PRINCIPLES:

Seeking Shalom is

_____

Seeking Shalom is mutual.

VIDEO

While viewing this week's first video, *"Seeking Shalom is Mutual,"* feel free to record any thoughts or ideas you find meaningful.

DISCUSSION

1. What do you think happens to charity or missions when done outside the context of relationships?

2. Do you have any examples of non-relational charity/missions?

3. Saying that we need to have relational models is one thing. Claiming they should be mutual is another. What is the difference, and why is that important?

4. How do you think this call to mutuality connects with the theme of image bearing?

RELATIONALITY reminds us that we have to _____ _____ and connect with those we desire to _____. Mutuality reminds us that _____ are in need of _____ too.

VIDEO

While viewing this week's second video, *"Seeking Shalom is Participatory,"* feel free to record any thoughts or ideas you find meaningful.

DISCUSSION

1. What happens when those experiencing poverty shift from being seen as recipients to being seen as participants?

2. What examples do you have of recipient-based frameworks and the effect they had?

3. Have you had an experience where being invited into a role of greater leadership or participation was transformative for you?

4. How does this concept of *participatory* relate either to the relational framework for understanding poverty or to the theme of image bearing?

IMAGE BEARING

What does it mean that all people are made in the image of God?

- **TO BE MADE** in the image of God means that humans were made with

  infinite _____.

- **TO BE MADE** in the image of God means that humans were made

  for _____.

- **TO BE MADE** in the image of God means that humans were made to

  be _____ with God.

BUILDING BLOCKS OF CHARITY

Consider *The Cold Water Collective* (see page 23 for the text). In the following diagram, write down in each quadrant how the item in that box (problem, solution, process, or success) was defined within the program, then discuss the following questions:

PROBLEM	SOLUTION
PROCESS	**SUCCESS**

1. Who defined each of the four parts?

2. Choose one of the four parts. What do you think would have been different if the recipients had been participants in that area from the beginning?

3. Describe what the Cold Water Collective program might have been like if it had been designed from beginning to end in a participatory manner.

PRAYER JOURNAL

Write out your own prayer for implementing the principle of *mutuality*, about how to enter into mutually transformative relationships with those you have previously sought only to serve.

Write out your own prayer for how to honor people as *participants* in creating, pursuing, and achieving Shalom.

REFLECTION QUESTIONS

1. Take a moment to look back over your notes from Day One: Class Day. What do you think are your most important takeaways from the fourth session?

2. In your own words, define and/or describe the first principle of seeking Shalom, *mutuality*.

3. In your own words, define and/or describe the second principle of seeking Shalom, *participatory*.

_____

_____

_____

_____

_____

_____

_____

4. Thinking about the meanings of image bearing that were highlighted this week, what words do you think would describe a ministry model that fully embodies all three (see page 81)?

_____

_____

_____

_____

_____

_____

_____

SCRIPTURE MEDITATION

1. Carefully read through 1 Corinthians 12:4-27.

2. Describe when you became aware of a spiritual gift and what it means for you when you get to exercise it on behalf of others.

_____

_____

_____

_____

_____

_____

3. How different would your life be now if someone had hindered you from using your gifts?

_____

_____

_____

_____

_____

_____

4. Although we may do it because we want to serve others and love them well, it is often easier to do things for others than to invite them to be full gift-bearing participants. How do you think we begin to shift that mindset?

5. Carefully reread the passage. As you read, prayerfully envision the people you have felt called to serve. Ask the Spirit to open your heart to their creative potential, their capacity, their giftedness. Pray to see them not through the lens of their deficiencies, but through the lens of their giftedness.

CASE STUDY

This week's Case Study will be on a ministry effort called *Growing Hope*. Read their story below and answer the questions that follow.

Growing Hope. Sam and Maria intentionally relocated to a low-income neighborhood in their city to be closer to those closest to the heart of God – the poor. After a year of living there, they had seen a number of things that burdened their hearts. Two in particular stood out. One, teenagers seemed to have nothing to do but stand on the sidewalk and get into trouble after school and on the weekends. Two, they were not pleased with the state of many of the yards and community areas in the neighborhood. There were a lot of unkempt yards, uncontrolled weeds, and litter. Sitting on their porch one night watching four teenagers wander past an empty, overgrown lot, one of them said, "They seem bored, what if we paid them to clean that lot right there?" The couple looked at each other and they both knew they'd just had an amazing idea! They talked to a few of the kids to see if they'd like to have a job in the neighborhood making some money – enough not only to spend on new clothes but also to save for college. The teens said that they did. The couple then went to every affluent church and Christian they knew to get donations for mowers, weed eaters, trimmers... the works. They came up with the business name and vision statement: *Growing Hope—Employing teens to grow beauty in their neighborhood and hope in their lives.* They got a logo designed and shirts made. They talked to friends who ran businesses about making this a legitimate company. Since the couple knew little about lawn care or landscaping, they found a donor who also was willing to take on Growing Hope as the "Boss" to hire teens, find projects, manage the work, etc. When they looked at the truck, the trailer of equipment, the shirts... they could hardly speak. Donors saw the pictures in the newsletter, read about their vision, and the donations flowed in! Sam and Maria couldn't contain their excitement over the difference it would make in the neighborhood and in the lives of the teenagers who worked with Growing Hope. After one summer, they had 5 teens working with them, mainly doing projects the funders were paying them to do. They are trying to find paying projects but think they may have to do all donor-based work in the neighborhood and seek paying work in the wealthier neighborhoods down the street.

1. What about this story captured your attention the most? Why?

2. Where do you see the traditional charity paradigm at work?

3. Filter this story through the lens of mutuality. Based on what you have learned about that Shalom principle, how does Growing Hope measure up to that idea? In what ways could they improve?

4. Filter this story through the lens of participatory. Based on what you have learned about that Shalom principle, how does Growing Hope measure up to that idea? In what ways could they improve?

5. If you could go back in time to when Sam and Maria first had this idea, what would you say to them?

6. If you were to come alongside and partner with Sam and Maria at this stage in the ministry, what would you want to do?

VIDEO

The Lupton Center has curated additional online video content exclusively available to Seeking Shalom participants. This week you have some really rich content available. You actually have two videos this week, each one spotlighting a specific person or ministry that embodies one of the principles from this week. You can choose to watch them both or just focus on the one that interests you the most.

To view this video, go to **LuptonCenter.org/SSResrouces** and use the password: **ShalomSeeker**.

The video options are: *"Session Four: Spotlight on Mutuality"* and *"Session Four: Spotlight on Participatory."* After watching the video, answer the questions below

QUESTIONS ON *MUTUALITY:*

1. What did you learn about the benefits of cultivating mutual relationships?

2. What did you learn about the challenges of cultivating mutual relationships?

_____

_____

_____

_____

_____

_____

_____

3. Do you feel more excited or nervous about cultivating mutual relationships with those you have sought to serve?

_____

_____

_____

_____

_____

_____

_____

_____

4. With whom has God placed on your heart to begin this journey? How might you get started?

QUESTIONS ON *PARTICIPATORY:*

1. What things about the Urban Recipe model stick out most to you? Why?

2. How would you compare or contrast this to other ministries that seek to address food insecurity?

3. What needs was Urban Recipe meeting that had nothing to do with food?

4. Why do you think this approach is so much more meaningful to those who are involved?

4. In what ways does this cause you to rethink ministries with which you are familiar?

HOW DO WE SEEK SHALOM? PART TWO

KEY IDEA

Shalom is an all-inclusive concept. No part of our lives or this world is exempt from God's vision of bringing about Shalom. Too often, attempts to engage poverty do so through single-issue models. For Shalom to be a reality, we must establish a more holistic view of people, the places in which they live, and the issues that they face. As we develop a more comprehensive view of what we seek to address, we are going to need to leverage more than hearts to get the work done. Seeking Shalom will mean engaging minds, skillsets, and expertise as well.

LEARNING OBJECTIVES:

• Participants will come understand that the journey to Shalom requires a holistic view of people, places, and the issues they face. A holistic, rather than a single-issue, approach allows people and communities to flourish.

• Participants will come to understand that the journey to Shalom demands more than compassion and generosity. Flourishing also requires assets, knowledge, skills, and expertise. The heart and the mind must be engaged in seeking Shalom.

> "I wish that instead of investing money in service, we would invest in development — business, housing, creating jobs, creating more sustainable efforts that the people themselves articulate they are interested in doing."
>
> **Noel Castellanos,** *President of CCDA & Author of* Where the Cross Meets the Street

"See, I have chosen Bezalel son of Uri, the son of Hur, of the tribe of Judah, and I have filled him with the Spirit of God, with wisdom, with understanding, with knowledge and with all kinds of skills to make artistic designs for work in gold, silver and bronze, to cut and set stones, to work in wood, and to engage in all kinds of crafts. Moreover, I have appointed Oholiab son of Ahisamak, of the tribe of Dan, to help him. Also I have given ability to all the skilled workers to make everything I have commanded you..."

- Exodus 31:2-6

THIS WEEK'S SHALOM PRINCIPLES:

SEEKING SHALOM is

_____

SEEKING SHALOM engages the

_____

VIDEO

While viewing this week's first video, *"Seeking Shalom is Holistic,"* feel free to record any thoughts or ideas you find meaningful.

DISCUSSION

1. Noel Castellanos mentioned that we have to know when to shift from a service model to a development model. What do you think that means?

2. Steve Corbett described the difference between holistic being understood as a reference to the nature of human beings versus a way of thinking about the interrelated sectors in a community. Why do you think both are important if our goal is Shalom?

3. The point of this video was to invite us to take a more comprehensive view of the people and communities in which we live. Why do you think we default to single-issue approaches to alleviating material poverty?

4. Think about a charity model in which you have participated that took this single-issue approach. What gaps were left by not seeing people as holistic or not having a holistic view of the context in which they lived?

NEHEMIAH: A PORTRAIT OF SHALOM

They said to me, "Those who survived the exile and are back in the province are in great trouble and disgrace. The wall of Jerusalem is broken down, and its gates have been burned with fire." - Nehemiah 1:3

- Repentance
- Reading of the law
- A summons to fast and pray
- People recommitting to obey the Lord
- Sharing of food with the hungry
- **Re-establishment of the infrastructure and the laws that governed society, a community re-creating itself**

THE FCS FLOURISHING NEIGHBORHOOD INDEX

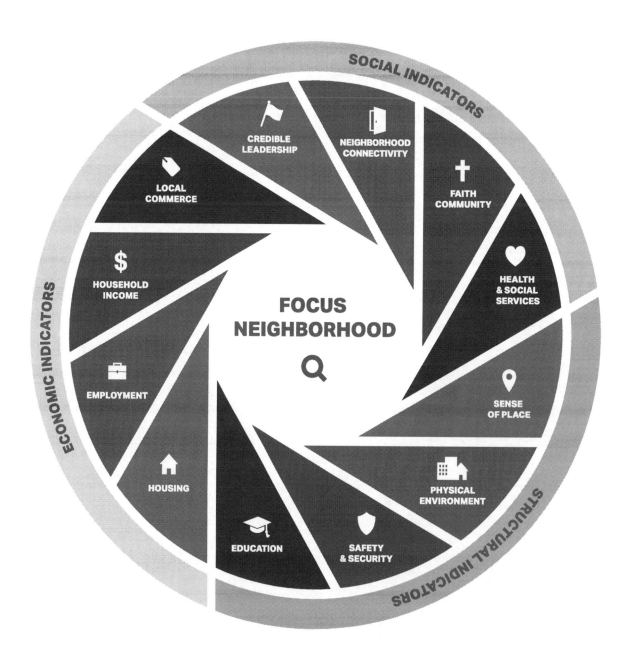

1. FCS | Focused Community Strategies used the index to gather data and do surveys as a means to both understand what needs to be addressed and measure progress along the way. It is a tool they use in their own community, as well as a tool used to train others who are trying to do holistic development in their context.

2. As you study this image of the FNI, which includes 12 indicators broken up into 3 categories, what strikes you about it?

_____

_____

_____

_____

3. What categories make the most sense to you when it comes to addressing chronic poverty?

_____

_____

_____

_____

4. Which ones make the least sense? Why?

_____

_____

_____

_____

5. Think about a community where you have worked to address a symptom of chronic poverty. It can be a domestic or a foreign context. Can you see how a lack of health in any of these indicators played a role in the material poverty that you witnessed there?

6. It is easy for us to connect material poverty to some of these categories — like jobs or income. How might an improvement in those factors still not disrupt chronic poverty if there is a lack of health in another category?

VIDEO

While viewing this week's second video, *"Seeking Shalom Engages the Mind,"* feel free to record any thoughts or ideas you find meaningful.

DISCUSSION

1. What did you think of the Carver Market — a grocery store in a food desert — as an example of leveraging the mind?

2. Can you think of and share an example of a charity or ministry in which you participated where skills and expertise were leveraged to create real and lasting change?

3. Can you think of an example of a charity or ministry that could be transformed if it were to engage people whose expertise related to the issue it is addressing?

ENGAGING THE MIND ALONGSIDE THE HEART

THE HEART leads us to _____ when we see

people _____ . The mind allows us to _____ with them in ways that makes

possible.

THE _____ we feel when witnessing a symptom of poverty is rightly attributed

to God's work in us. If we want to address the causes of poverty, we will also need to see _____

knowledge and expertise as gifts of God's Spirit.

What do you think?

_____

_____

_____

_____

_____

_____

_____

_____

_____

GOD HAS...

- [ ] **A HEART FOR THE POOR**
- [ ] **A MIND FOR THE POOR**
- [ ] **ALL OF THE ABOVE**

PRAYER JOURNAL

Write out your own prayer for embracing a more holistic vision for people, places, and the issues we face.

_____

_____

_____

_____

_____

Write out your own prayer for engaging the mind alongside the heart when addressing the challenges your community is facing.

_____

_____

_____

_____

_____

_____

REFLECTION QUESTIONS

1. Take a moment to look back over your notes from Day One: Class Day. What do you think are your most important takeaways from the fifth session?

2. In your own words, define and/or describe the first principle of seeking Shalom, *holistic*.

3. In your own words, define and/or describe the second principle of seeking Shalom, *engaging the mind.*

_____

_____

_____

_____

_____

_____

_____

4. Compassion can cause us to respond to the suffering of others with lots of generosity and with little hesitation. In crises, this is a good and beautiful thing. It saves lives. In cases of chronic poverty, however, this rapid compassion can get misapplied, leading to ineffective or harmful actions. Based on what you have learned about the principles for seeking Shalom, what should happen after the need is seen and before people spring into action?

_____

_____

_____

_____

_____

_____

SCRIPTURE MEDITATION

1. Carefully read Genesis 41:28-38 & 46-49.

2. Joseph's story is a fascinating example of how God's activity and human skill can combine to bring about a creative strategy to address serious human need. Whether it was in prison or in his role of authority in Egypt, Joseph sought to be attuned to what God was doing and willingly used his knowledge and expertise to solve problems.

3. In what ways do you sense God's activity in your community?

4. How might God use your role or your skill set to join in God's work in your community?

5. Spend time praying for sensitivity to what God is actively doing in your community to bring about Shalom. Pray carefully about your own role and your own gifts. Pray that you will remain available to participate in what God is doing in your community.

CASE STUDY

This week's Case Study will be a little different. Rather than describing an existing ministry, you are presented with the opportunity to step in at the moment when the needs have come to the surface, before any actions have been taken. Read the story and then answer the questions that follow.

You have just moved to the community of Clifton, a town of 25,000 on the outskirts of a major metropolitan area. The subdivision in which you live, the schools your kids attend, your place of work, as well as your church are all filled with mostly middle-class professionals and their families. Safe, quiet, and community-focused, you are pleased with your new home. However, it doesn't take long before you discover there are parts of the community that look significantly different from your own. Driving through town, you notice there is a concentration of poverty in one particular area. You see the names of schools that you have heard are struggling. You find out that there are a number of homeless families whose kids attend there. You also observe a number of vacant homes and a lack of businesses. You can't help noticing these economic lines also follow racial ones. You feel called by God to respond compassionately to those on the margins. You find out that for years, organizations have been providing resources and services to meet the needs of residents here — lunches in the summer for kids, rent and utilities assistance, public transportation passes, a food pantry, and a clothing closet. It appears that these things have not made a significant impact on poverty in the area.

1. What would you do? Where would you start?

2. Who would you involve?

3. What would you like to know that you don't know?

4. If you were to start an initiative/program, what would you focus on?
    How would you go about addressing this?

VIDEO

The Lupton Center has curated additional online video content available exclusively to Seeking Shalom participants. This week you will watch a TEDxTalk from The Lupton Center's Director, Dr. Shawn Duncan.

To view this video, go to **LuptonCenter.org/SSResrouces** and use the password: **ShalomSeeker**. Choose the video entitled, *"Session Five: Changing Charity for Good."*

After watching the video answer the questions below.

1. What did you think about how the "teach a man to fish" proverb was reframed in this presentation?

2. The video set up a contrast between foreign service trips that make for good stories versus business strategies that make for sustainable models. In the service trip model, the outsiders tend to be the heroes, whereas in the development approach, the community and its assets get highlighted. Can you think of some good stories from short-term charity that likely had a negative impact in the long-term?

3. If you have ever served in the developing world, how might a long-term business strategy (like the yucca farming example in the video) in that context lead to real and lasting change?

_____

_____

_____

_____

_____

_____

_____

4. As you think about the contexts in which you are currently witnessing chronic poverty, what are the skill sets and expertise that could be engaged to bring about creative solutions?

_____

_____

_____

_____

_____

_____

_____

WHAT NOW?

KEY IDEA

To seek Shalom means that we are not content with simply alleviating suffering. We want to see real, lasting, and meaningful change occur in people's lives and in their communities. In other words, seeking Shalom means we have to care about impact, not just activity. Shalom means measuring more than the things we did with good intentions. Shalom means measuring what those actions have accomplished.

LEARNING OBJECTIVES:

• Participants will come to understand that healthy models will measure impact, not just activity

• Participants will practice diagnosing a charity model using the core concepts learned in *Seeking Shalom*

"The measurement question is huge, and it has to be dealt with. Our hearts, minds, and the money will follow what we measure. So we have to stop measuring brokenness."

Peter Block, *Author,* Community, The Structure of Belonging

"Seek the Shalom of the city to which I have carried you into exile. Pray to the Lord for it, because if it experiences Shalom, you too will experience Shalom." - Jeremiah 29:7

THIS WEEK'S SHALOM PRINCIPLE

SEEKING SHALOM means we will measure _____, not just activity.

VIDEO

While viewing this week's first video, *"Seeing Shalom Measures Impact,"* feel free to record any thoughts or ideas you find meaningful.

DISCUSSION

1. The video contrasted activity versus measuring impact. What are some examples that you would give of the differences between these two?

2. Sometimes we resist putting measurements on charity or mission. Why do you think that is?

3. When you do hear metrics from a charity or mission effort being celebrated, what do they tend to talk about? What aspect of these numbers might be a picture of health? How might they tell an incomplete story?

4. Peter Block, veteran community development practitioner, described the difference between measuring brokenness and measuring well-being and assets. Why do you think we tend to measure the former?

5. Atlanta Mission was highlighted in the video. There was a significant shift in moving from measuring graduation rates to measuring an individual's growth in five key areas. What struck you about their story?

6. Even if you are not working with people experiencing homelessness, what did Atlanta Mission model that is helpful for you?

GOD IS MAKING ALL THINGS NEW

Isaiah 65:17-19: "See, I will create **new** heavens and a new earth. The **former things will not be remembered**, nor will they come to mind. But be glad and rejoice forever in what I will create, for I will create Jerusalem to be a delight and its people a joy. I will rejoice over Jerusalem and take delight in my people; the sound of weeping and of crying will be heard in it **no more**."

Matthew 6:9-13: "This, then, is how you should pray: 'Our Father in heaven, hallowed be your name, your kingdom come, your will be done, **on earth as it is in heaven**. Give us today our daily bread. And forgive us our debts, as we also have forgiven our debtors. And lead us not into temptation, but deliver us from the evil one.'"

Matthew 19:28-30: Jesus said to them, "Truly I tell you, at the **renewal of all things**, when the Son of Man sits on his glorious throne, you who have followed me will also sit on twelve thrones, judging the twelve tribes of Israel. And everyone who has left houses or brothers or sisters or father or mother or wife or children or fields for my sake will receive a hundred times as much and will inherit eternal life. But many who are first will be last, and many who are last will be first."

Luke 4:17-20: And the scroll of the prophet Isaiah was handed to him. Unrolling it, he found the place where it is written: "The Spirit of the Lord is on me, because he has anointed me to proclaim good news to the poor. He has sent me to proclaim **freedom** for the prisoners and **recovery** of sight for the blind, to set the oppressed **free**, to proclaim the year of the Lord's favor." Then he rolled up the scroll, gave it back to the attendant and sat down. The eyes of everyone in the synagogue were fastened on him.

Ephesians 1:9-10: And he made known to us the mystery of his will according to his good pleasure, which he purposed in Christ, to be put into effect when the times reach their fulfillment—to bring **unity to all things** in heaven and on earth under Christ.

VIDEO

While viewing this week's second video, which is an animation of all five principles we have covered, feel free to record any thoughts or ideas you find meaningful.

Mutuality

Participatory

Holistic

Mind

Impact

EXERCISE – CASE STUDY: A DIAGNOSTIC

CASE STUDY, PART ONE: INITIAL REACTIONS

1. Unless the Case Study was read aloud to the class as a whole, go to the page instructed by the Facilitator and read the Case Study aloud in your Circle.

2. What are your initial reactions about this ministry?

_____

_____

_____

_____

_____

3. What seems to be the most promising part of this model?

_____

_____

_____

_____

_____

4. What concerns you the most?

_____

_____

_____

_____

_____

_____

_____

5. What terms or concepts from our study of *Seeking Shalom* came to mind as you heard this Case Study read?

_____

_____

_____

_____

_____

_____

_____

_____

CASE STUDY, PART TWO: RANKING THE FIVE

On your own, go through each of the five principles and rate them on a scale of 1 to 5. After you have done this, share your rankings with each other and then discuss the questions to consider.

1. Mutuality

A "1" means it is completely "us-them" with clear distinctions between the givers and the receivers and a "5" means there is an authentic "we" with real reciprocity, where everyone is benefitting from each other.

Question to Consider: To what degree do you think this ministry suffers from a proximity disorder?

2. Participatory

A "1" means there is one group doing everything for another group and a "5" means that everything is done *with* all people as equal participants in the work.

Question to Consider: To what degree do you think this ministry embodies the belief that the materially poor are bearers of God's image?

3. Holistic

A "1" means that it is a single-issue problem with a single-solution strategy and a "5" means that there is a comprehensive understanding of the interrelated factors creating the problem, as well as a multi-layered approach to addressing it.

Question to Consider: To what degree is this ministry rooted in the relational framework for understanding poverty (see page 40)?

1   2   3   4   5

4. Mind

A "1" means that it strictly engages emotional responses to alleviating the pain caused by poverty and a "5" means that the best expertise is being leveraged to create lasting solutions to poverty.

Question to Consider: How well has this ministry distinguished between crisis and chronic and worked to create robust development-based approaches where chronic poverty is present?

1   2   3   4   5

5. **Impact**

A "1" means that the success metrics measure volume of resources distributed or amount of activity done and a "5" means that it measures the end results of the work so as to create real, lasting change.

Question to Consider: Do you think this ministry is designed to alleviate the pain people experience due to poverty (a symptoms approach) or to address the causes of poverty (a systems approach)?

CASE STUDY, PART THREE: THE FOUR PARTS OF CHARITY

Determine how the ministry being studied would define each of the four building blocks of charity by discussing the questions listed in each quadrant.

PROBLEM

- Is the problem defined based on the symptoms or the causes of poverty?

- What voices or information are missing from this understanding of the problem?

- How might their understanding of the problem lead to ineffective or harmful results?

SOLUTION

- Is the solution a lasting solution, or does it provide perpetual help to a perpetually recurring need?

- Who determined that this model was the right response?

- In what ways might this understanding of the solution lead to ineffective or harmful results?

PROCESS

- Does the process involve the materially poor as recipients or as participants?

- Who makes decisions, determines strategies, and sets objectives?

- In what ways might the process itself hinder effectiveness of solving the problem?

SOLUTION

- Are the metrics based on the work or generosity of the helpers or on what is happening in those it is intended to benefit?

- Who gets to decide what is measured, what stories are shared with supporters, and what milestones are celebrated?

- How might the metrics being used actually hinder this ministry from doing healthy work?

CASE STUDY, PART FOUR: PROPOSING A NEW MODEL/VISION CASTING

Now that you have had a chance to diagnose the model that currently exists, spend some time casting a vision for a healthier, more effective approach that this ministry could take. Describe its key components below.

CASE STUDY, PART FIVE: THE CHANGE PROCESS

Critiquing an existing model and coming up with ideas for a new one may prove easy in comparison to the actual process of leading the change from the ways things are to the way things could be. What would you suggest as the leaders' first three steps for the change process?

1

2

3

PRAYER JOURNAL

Write out your own prayer for those you have journeyed with these last six weeks, that they may experience Shalom and participate with God in seeking the Shalom of their city.

REFLECTION QUESTIONS

As you come to the close of the Seeking Shalom curriculum, it is important to take hold of the key things God has revealed to you so that your life can actively seek Shalom in your **day-to-day context**. For the review exercise this final week, you are being asked to not only flip through the class notes from Session Six, but also to take the time to skim from the beginning of your Participant's Guide. On this page, write down the top two or three most important takeaways from this whole experience **as it relates to your own life personally**. On the following page, you will be asked to write down takeaways that connect to any ministries in which you participate. For now, though, focus on what God most desires for you to apply to your own life.

As you come to the close of the Seeking Shalom curriculum, it is important to take hold of the key things God has revealed to you so that you can actively seek Shalom **in the ministries** in which you are involved. On this page, write down the top two or three most important takeaways from this whole experience **as it relates to your ministry context**. On the previous page, you were asked to write down takeaways that connect to you personally. Now you can shift your focus to what God most desires for you to apply to any ministries in which you participate.

SCRIPTURE MEDITATION

Carefully read this passage. Keep your heart and mind open to how the Spirit is revealing God's radically generous ways.

Deuteronomy 15:1-15: At the end of every seven years you must cancel debts. This is how it is to be done: Every creditor shall cancel any loan they have made to a fellow Israelite. They shall not require payment from anyone among their own people, because the Lord's time for canceling debts has been proclaimed. You may require payment from a foreigner, but you must cancel any debt your fellow Israelite owes you. However, there need be no poor people among you, for in the land the Lord your God is giving you to possess as your inheritance, he will richly bless you, if only you fully obey the Lord your God and are careful to follow all these commands I am giving you today. For the Lord your God will bless you as he has promised, and you will lend to many nations but will borrow from none. You will rule over many nations but none will rule over you. If anyone is poor among your fellow Israelites in any of the towns of the land the Lord your God is giving you, do not be hardhearted or tightfisted toward them. Rather, be openhanded and freely lend them whatever they need. Be careful not to harbor this wicked thought: "The seventh year, the year for canceling debts, is near," so that you do not show ill will toward the needy among your fellow Israelites and give them nothing. They may then appeal to the Lord against you, and you will be found guilty of sin. Give generously to them and do so without a grudging heart; then because of this the Lord your God will bless you in all your work and in everything you put your hand to. There will always be poor people in the land. Therefore I command you to be openhanded toward your fellow Israelites who are poor and needy in your land. If any of your people—Hebrew men or women—sell themselves to you and serve you six years, in the seventh year you must let them go free. And when you release them, do not send them away empty-handed. Supply them liberally from your flock, your threshing floor and your winepress. Give to them as the Lord your God has blessed you. Remember that you were slaves in Egypt and the Lord your God redeemed you. That is why I give you this command today.

After prayerfully reading Deut 15:1-15, respond to the following reflection questions.

1. Why did God have the expectation that there should be no poor person among them?

2. Do you think this is possible today? Do you think if God's people lived with radical generosity like this, material poverty could be eradicated in your city?

PRAYER JOURNAL

3. Write out a prayer for the hearts and minds of God's people in your city to be drawn to embody God's radical generosity.

_____

_____

_____

_____

_____

_____

_____

_____

_____

_____

_____

4. God commands them to be openhanded. Do you feel like this describes you? Write out a prayer that God may loosen your grip on things that could be used to restore and redeem your neighbors.

_____

_____

_____

_____

5. God bases this call to eradicate poverty and practice radical generosity on the fact that God redeemed them from Egypt and has blessed them in the Promised Land. Write out a prayer for God to open your heart and mind to all God has done to redeem and bless you. Pray that God will use that to make you generous, as God is generous.

CONTINUING THE JOURNEY

Wow, what a journey! Thank you for opening your heart and mind to the ways in which God is calling you and your community to participate with God in seeking the Shalom of your city. Would you consider continuing the journey by inviting others to join you? Here are a three ideas for you to consider:

1. **Lead Your Own Group.** Would you be willing to lead your own *Seeking Shalom* small-group experience? If so, who do you think you should invite to join you? When would you like to start? You might consider grabbing another participant from your small group to co-lead with you to expand the awareness of these frameworks in your context.

2. **Come for a Visit.** Would you consider bringing a group from your ministry context to visit FCS | Focused Community Strategies in Atlanta? A few times a year, The Lupton Center hosts a two-day Open House event at FCS to introduce people to Christian Community Development, to our neighborhood, and to how we are seeking the Shalom of our city. Check out **LuptonCenter.org** for more information.

3. **Host an Event.** Would you consider hosting a seminar in your community? You may not be able to get all the other local churches and nonprofits to join you for all six weeks of *Seeking Shalom*, but you may be able to entice them to come to an evening entitled "Reimagine Charity." This is the Lupton Center's dynamic and interactive seminar that introduces people to the frameworks covered in *Seeking Shalom*. Hosting an event like this could be a great way to get people in your city talking about how you can work together for the Shalom of your community. Check our **LuptonCenter.org** for more information.

GLOSSARY

Activity Measures (or Program Measures) - These are measures related to the outputs of an organization's programs — volunteer hours, events held, number of participants in a program, pounds of food distributed, amount of bus passes given away, etc. These do not measure outcomes, or actual change in any one person, family, or community's life. *Activity* is what the organization is doing, not the impact it is having.

Agency - Charity is dangerous when it does not involve the ideas, desires, abilities, or input of those it is intended to benefit. This lack of inclusion is a denial of the agency of the materially poor, which is the will, right, and desire to govern their own lives.

Asset-Based Community Development - The ABCD movement considers local assets as the primary building blocks of sustainable community development. Building on the skills of local residents, the power of local associations, and the supportive functions of local institutions, ABCD draws upon existing community strengths to build stronger, more sustainable communities for the future. This is in contrast to a deficiency mindset that bases the work on what people/places are lacking.

Compassion - In Scripture, compassion literally means "to suffer with," and it is a term that theologically points to solidarity, engagement, and personal encounter. However, it is used in our day mostly as a descriptor for the feelings of pity one has when seeing someone in material need. When compassion is used as a critique in this series, it is this latter connotation being addressed. It has become shorthand for a "heart-only" approach to engaging material poverty.

Community Development - When organizations transition from a relief model to a development model, they often think only in terms of the person or the family. Developing the capacities of an individual through job readiness training, budgeting classes, or counseling is extremely important work. Development, though, also needs to be applied to the environments in which people and their families live. There will be limited results for a person whose individual capacities are being strengthened while living in an unhealthy environment. Neighborhoods matter. Community Development seeks to address place, not just people. It works on infrastructure, housing, business creation and jobs, educational and political systems, local civic associations, etc. Community Development wants to ensure that there are places where people and their families can flourish in God's Shalom. The Christian Community Development Association (ccda.org) was founded approximately 30 years ago to promote a biblically-based and Gospel-centered approach to Community Development. When not rooted in the way of

Jesus, Community Development can prioritize those with privilege and wealth and end up displacing lower income families and erasing the history and identity of a neighborhood. Christian Community Development says that those placed on society's margins are at the center of God's concern, and the work of restoring neighborhoods should put their interests first.

Crisis vs. Chronic Poverty - When this distinction is missed or ignored, it creates toxic charity. Crisis poverty is brought on by unexpected, uncontrollable external forces like a hurricane, loss of income, or debilitating illness. In a crisis situation, the immediate, short-term provision of resources from one group to another can be life-saving. Chronic poverty, however, is long-standing, multifaceted, and complex. A one-way distribution of material resources (ie. relief) cannot solve this problem. It requires a development response. Applying relief strategies to address chronic poverty is at best ineffective and is often harmful. See also "Relief vs. Development"

Development - See "Relief vs. Development."

Dignity - All people have been made in the image of God, which means they have inherent worth. It also means they have inherent capacity — abilities, ideas, assets, solutions, etc. To define a person by their deficiencies or to treat them as a passive recipient of someone else's help rejects dignity. Dignity means we involve everyone as participants, as equals. Everyone's voice is heard, everyone's gifts are utilized.

Direct Service (or, Household Services) vs. Development - Direct services are programs that address a felt need with a material resource to provide relief to that symptomatic problem. These are sometimes called household services because they are not thinking at a level other than what needs exist for a specific household (rent, food, utilities, school supplies, transportation, etc.). Development is concerned with what is causing the felt need and works to strengthen the capacities of the individual and/or the community to solve the root problem.

Disempower - When charity is set up to perpetually provide for others, it is disempowering because it does not leverage their gifts, ideas, and capacities. By not actively involving their assets, it progressively weakens both individuals and communities.

Economy of Neighborliness vs Acquisitiveness - This concept includes but is not limited to the financial understanding of the word economy. An economy of neighborliness refers to a community that is structured around rules, rituals, and habits that protect and promote community, the common good. In contrast, an economy of acquisitiveness has its fundamental purpose the acquiring of more for one's own personal safety and prosperity without regard for how it affects others. In the former, we are citizens and neighbors. In the latter, we are consumers. In the former, we seek the formation of a beloved community. In the latter we seek independent wealth. The former seeks the good of all. The latter protects the rights of the individual to gain, grow, and consume.

Enable vs. Empower - We can create systems that enable the problem to persist or empower people and communities to thrive. By doing things FOR others, we enable the problem to continue. By doing things WITH each other, we empower communities to thrive. Enabling weakens people, communities, and their systems. Empowering enhances and leverages existing assets so that individuals and communities grow, develop, and thrive.

Episodic vs. Systemic Poverty - This distinction refers to a common misunderstanding by the materially wealthy of the nature of material poverty. It is often assumed that the experience of poverty is about one moment, one need, one issue, etc., and can be addressed with one solution. It is, in other words, episodic. The reality for most facing material poverty, however, is that it is systemic. There are a myriad of causes, multiple dimensions to each need, and a series of compounding effects.

Generous Solidarity (or Neighborly Fidelity) - This is shorthand for the kind of relationships God intended for us to experience. The biblical framework is one of a community living in covenant with God, each other, and the systems that establish their shared life. God intended that people live knowing that they belonged to one another. Life is not the pursuit of individual freedom or success. It is about participating in community with a commitment to each other and to building a deeply generous economy.

Holistic - This term is used in two important but distinct ways. One is in reference to individuals as holistic beings, which means you can't compartmentalize a person into spiritual, physical, emotional, vocational, etc. To move toward flourishing, all parts of a person must be addressed because they all affect each other. The other use of holistic is in reference to whole communities and the complex web of economic, civic, educational, business, environmental, etc. systems that contribute to (or prevent) flourishing. This is what is meant by integrated or comprehensive community development. Seeking Shalom requires holism in both senses of the word.

Image Bearer - Every person is made in the image of God, which means they have dignity, worth, and capacity (See "Dignity" above). As image bearers, we cannot experience Shalom unless we are using our gifts as co-laborers with God in bringing about flourishing. Restoring people as image bearers, not providing for them, is how we seek Shalom.

Impact Measures (or Population Measures) - These are measures that look at the actual outcomes work is having upon the people and communities being served. It is looking at well-being, vitality, and flourishing. It is asking whether or not people are better off than they were before. It is considering if sustainable independence is being developed. These metrics guide organizations that want to see real and lasting change and are willing to adapt what they are doing for the highest possible impact.

Incarnation - This is both a theological and a methodological framework for seeking Shalom. God put on flesh and moved into the neighborhood (John 1, MSG). Jesus is relational, not transactional, in the work of redemption. Healthy models will prioritize proximity and relationship. Models are unhealthy when there is a geographic and relational distance between those those who seek to help and those who are supposed to benefit. The posture and practice of incarnation guides us towards mutuality, which allows us to more fully understand the nature of the challenges being faced and the possible solutions that can exist.

Infrastructures of Shalom - This phrase points to the need to weave the dignity of people — and the assurance of their access to networks, resources, and opportunities — into the very fabric of how our communities are organized, governed, and supported, so that all can   flourish together.

Integrated (or Comprehensive) Community Development - See "Holistic"

Internalized Oppression - When there are repeated, external messages from majority culture — direct or indirect — about the inferiority of a marginalized group, these messages eventually get internalized in ways that cause an oppressed group not only to believe these messages but also to act according to the stereotypes projected onto them.

Jubilee - God never intended generational poverty to exist. God legislated the practice of Jubilee, which was the legal, systemic return of land and inheritance to its original owners. It is the canceling of debts. It is the setting free of those oppressed. Jubilee restores equal footing and participation in God's community of generosity and sustainability (Lev 25:8-13).

GLOSSARY

Materially Poor - Poverty affects all people regardless of their income level. This phrase is a deliberate choice not to assume the "poor" are those who have lower income levels. There are all kinds of poverty — emotional, relational, spiritual, vocational, etc. The materially poor refers to those who lack access to the necessary resources or systems for sustainable well-being.

Micro-Aggressions - It is obviously harmful when there are direct negative or derogatory statements made toward the materially poor. It is just as harmful, however, when there are indirect actions, words, or assumptions that communicate an inferior status of those with lower incomes. Whether intentional or unintentional, they are oppressive and harmful.

Mutuality - This is the practiced awareness that we belong to one another. Our income level does not define the extent of our needs. The materially well-off and the materially poor need one another. Shalom happens in the context of reconciled community, where interdependence is the antidote to systems that promote either dependence or independence.

One-Way vs. Reciprocal Giving - One-way giving means that one person or group sustains a system of freely giving a physical resource to another person or group. The beneficiary is not involved in any way other than receiving the material good. In one-way giving there is a clear distinction between who is the one in need and who is in the role of provider. Reciprocal giving, however, is a system where both parties need one another and benefit from each other. Everyone's gifts and everyone's needs are taken into account. There is no hierarchy of giver-receiver. It is a system of mutual, legitimate exchange.

Othering - This term refers to a use of language to categorize and distance oneself from another people group. It is the use of labels to define people based on race, gender, income level, etc. as a way to lessen them and to avoid seeing them as distinct, dignified individual with unique capacity. It perpetuates an us-them way of thinking and behaving.

Outcomes vs Outputs - An output is an activity measure. It is something we have done or ways that people have participated in something we have done. These are important and useful measures, but they are not definitive. An outcome is an impact measure. It looks at the actual success (or lack thereof) of the work being done. It is asking whether or not real and lasting change is being created.

Participatory Systems - This means that everything — from the way the problem is understood to how the solution is defined, how the procedures are developed, and how success is measured — is done with the full engagement of the materially poor.

Paternalistic Charity - This type of charity is a system that is set up to perpetually do for someone else what they have the capacity to do for themselves. It defines someone else's problem for them and executes the solution on their behalf.

Population Measures - See "Impact Measures"

Poverty Industry - The complex web of programs, services, institutions, products, and service providers that benefit more from the perpetuation of their own organizations than they do from creating real and lasting change in communities experiencing material poverty.

Poverty of Condition - A reference to deficiency of material resources. It is too often the sole focus of charity. Unless it is a crisis, the poverty of condition is a symptom of more important issues. Charity too often focuses solely or disproportionately upon the poverty of condition.

Program Measures - See "Activity Measures"

Proximity Disorder - The relational and geographic distance that separates those "serving" from those "being served." It prevents a healthy, accurate understanding of the problems and the possibility of creating a legitimate path forward.

Reciprocity - See "One-Way vs. Reciprocal Giving"

Relief vs. Development - This distinction refers to the responses applied to crisis vs. chronic poverty. Crisis requires relief. It is about ensuring that the basic needs to sustain human life and prevent continued disaster are met (water, food, shelter, medicine, etc.) Chronic poverty demands development, which is about restoring the systems that lead to sustainable well-being (roads, jobs, businesses, education, income-generating activities, etc.). Communities cannot thrive by perpetually depending upon outside charity to get by. Development repairs or creates the systems that allow communities to flourish as they leverage their own assets.

Second Disaster - In international development, this is a term that refers to the influx of unneeded supplies to a country/community following a natural disaster. The resources themselves, the expense of processing them, and the disruption they cause to traffic and infrastructure during a crisis is what makes this a second disaster. The unnecessary goods are often referred to as "SWEDOW" (see below).

Shalom - Some of the other phrases used to define Shalom in this series are: Holistic well-being; God's design; peace with God, self, others, the created order; flourishing economically, practically, and on a neighborhood level; harmoniously organized neighborhood; sustainable access to health and wholeness; prosperity in physical, spiritual, communal, etc. areas of life. Shalom is the comprehensive experience of flourishing within individuals and their communities.

Short-term Charity - Programs that are set up to meet immediate, felt needs but do not to address the cause of that need. It brings short-term relief from the pain of the symptom but does not change the condition long-term.

Silo Approach - Only addressing one issue without an awareness of, conversation with, or partnership alongside other agencies addressing related issues.

Social Marginalization - Being outside the systems of well-being that allow one to determine, through one's own work and initiative, one's well-being. If one is socially marginalized, hard work does not automatically lead to well-being. Low wages, unfair housing practices, lack of access to capital, disconnection from social networks of influence, prejudicial treatment by the legal system, lack of access to affordable resources for physical health, etc. are examples of being socially marginalized.

Social Ventriloquism - Marginalized people groups are often not listened to or taken as seriously as individuals from a dominant class or race. This decreased credibility may mean that when lower-income minority groups need to present ideas or make requests for partnership, they may choose to send their message through the mouth of an affluent, majority-culture person.

Sustainable Well-Being - Poverty is not alleviated, for example, by giving away cups of water to the thirsty. Poverty is alleviated, instead, when there is a living stream of water that is clean, affordable, and accessible to the whole community. Development establishes systems that create wealth in a sustainable fashion.

SWEDOW - "Stuff We Don't Want." A term used in the aid and charity industry for all of the second-hand giveaways that are donated to communities that have experienced a crisis or are known to be areas of chronic poverty. Though the intentions may be right, SWEDOW is the wrong resource at the wrong time given in the wrong way.

Symptoms and Causes - Material poverty is always a symptom of something else. There is a vast array of complex and interrelated causes. Seeking Shalom requires that we engage at the cause level.

Transactional Charity - Charity that is based on the exchange of a material resource. One person has a need. Another person has a resource. The one in need performs some action and receives that resource. No real relationship is formed.

Toxic Charity - This is the title of Dr. Bob Lupton's best-selling book *Toxic Charity: How Churches and Charities Hurt Those They Help...And How To Reverse It*. It is also shorthand for well intentioned efforts to love and serve the materially poor that do more harm than good.

Made in the USA
Lexington, KY
05 February 2018